AF428388

DO ALL BIRDS FLY?

ANIMAL BOOK FOR CHILDREN
CHILDREN'S ANIMAL BOOKS

Speedy Publishing LLC

40 E. Main St. #1156

Newark, DE 19711

www.speedypublishing.com

Copyright © 2017

All Rights reserved. No part of this book may be reproduced or used in any way or form or by any means whether electronic or mechanical, this means that you cannot record or photocopy any material ideas or tips that are provided in this book

Have you ever wondered whether or not all birds can fly? Or, how they are able to fly?

In this book, you will learn what makes an animal a bird, how they are able to fly, and about the different types of birds, including the flightless birds.

The ostrich, a species of large flightless birds native to Africa, the only living member of the genus Struthio, which is in the ratite family.

NOT ALL BIRDS CAN FLY

Even if they have wings and feathers, not all birds have the ability to fly. There are many different flightless birds, including the Penguin, Kakapo, Weka, Moa, Ostriches and Kiwi. You are probably most familiar with the penguin. The Penguin spends most of its time in water and they are known to be terrific swimmers. On the other hand, ostriches are very quick runners, with the ability to run faster than the horse that might be chasing it.

Weka bird. The endemic flightless birds in New Zealand.

Kiwis for Kiwi, is an independent charity which protects the New Zealand Kiwi population. They believe there are more types of flightless birds in their country than in other countries.

Little spotted kiwi, native to New Zealand

The kakapo, also called owl parrot, is a species of large, flightless, nocturnal, ground-dwelling parrot of the super-family Strigopoidea endemic to New Zealand

WHY CAN'T SOME BIRDS FLY

Referred to as flightless birds, these are birds that have lost their ability to fly through evolution. They consist of more than 60 species, such as the penguins and the ratites (consisting of the kiwi, rhea, cassowary, emu, and ostrich). The Inaccessible Island rail is the smallest of the flightless birds, with a length of 12.5cm and a weight of 34.7g. The ostrich is the largest (tallest and heaviest) with a height of 2.7m and a weight of 156kg. The ostrich is farmed for its decorative feathers, meat, and skins. Their skins are used to make leather. Have you ever seen an ostrich purse or ostrich leather belt?

Rhea (Rhea Americana) with fluffy feathers, Pantanal, Brazil

The domestic chicken is just one of the domesticated birds that have lost their ability to fly for an extended amount of time. However, its ancestors, the Mallard and the Red Junglefowl have the ability to fly for a long period of time.

Different birds have evolved to flightlessness independently and for different reasons. The Phorusrhacidae, which is now extinct, is a family of birds evolving to become a formidable terrestrial predator. The extinct family of terror birds (including their relatives the bathornithids), gastornithiforms, eogruids, and dromornithids, evolved into similar shapes (big heads, long necks, and long legs), even though they were not closely related.

They also shared traits of being flightless birds that were giant in size, with long legs, long necks, and vestigial wings with some species of the ratites, even though they were not related.

Cassowary Bird

Flock of emperor penguins walk down beach to waters edge

EXAMPLES OF FLIGHTLESS BIRDS

As you read earlier, the ostrich is known for its speed. Its legs are powerful enough that it can reach a speed of 40 miles per hour! They also use their legs to attack a predator. It has the ability to kick powerful enough that it can kill a lion. However, most of the time it will simply use its speed to outrun the threat of death by an enemy. They are also known for their size, as they can grow to be 9 feet tall.

Ostrich on the african savannah

They do not actually place their head into the ground as you may have seen in a cartoon. They actually lie down and place their neck and head to the ground so as to hide from a predator. You can only see their body from a distance and it only appears that they have placed their head into the ground.

The penguin is known as one of the most loved animals of the world. They are mostly located in the southern hemisphere. While we may think of the penguin as living in a very cold climate, such as Antarctica, they can also be found in a more temperate area such as South Africa, Australia, and the Galapagos Islands. The penguin uses its flippers similar to how a bird uses its wings, to propel and guide their bodies like torpedoes through water to evade predators and catch fish. You might say they fly like a bird, but it is in water rather than in the air. Many birds lost their power of flight, including the island species. On a small island, the ability to fly might be a disadvantage if likely to be blown by a storm out to sea.

Pair of chinstrap penguins, one buried in snow, other one standing above him

Another species is the emu, which is second only to the ostrich in size. Generally, females are slightly bigger than the males and wider across their rump. The largest emu can grow to 150 – 190 cm in height. From their bill to their tail, their length can range from 139 to 164 cm, with the male's average of 148.5 cm and a female average of 156.8 cm. Their weight can range from 18 to 60 kg, the average weight being between 31.5 and 37 kg in the males and the females, respectively.

Emus are the second largest member of the ratite group of flightless birds

Mononykus - they were a form of therapods, a carnivorous
dinosaur that lived in Mongolia in the Cretaceous Period.
Mononykus were transitional from dinosaur to bird.

WHAT MAKES AN ANIMAL A BIRD?

Its main characteristic is its feathers. There is no other animal that has feathers. Additional features which are important to birds are its hollow bones and its wings. They also lay eggs, similar to reptiles, but they are warm-blooded like mammals. The temperature of their body remains the same no matter how cold or hot the temperature is outside. This allows them to maintain a high energy level which is necessary for flying. There are over 9,000 different species of birds.

Gentoo Penguin jumping in the water

Homing pigeons

DIFFERENT TYPES OF BIRDS

You will see birds of all different sizes. Ostriches are some of the largest, and hummingbirds are one of the smallest. Different species eat different food. Some might feed on plants, some eat insects, while others might eat animals like rodents, snakes or fish. They are also well known for their magnificent migrating patterns. Some fly to a warmer climate for survival. Birds can also be pets, such as the tropical parrot. They have also been known to assist humans with varying tasks. The homing pigeon can carry a message and falcons are great hunters.

The incredibly beautiful Green Violet Eared
Hummingbird in the central mountains of Mexico.

Rooster feathers

THEIR FEATHERS

Their feathers have several functions: for flight, for regulation of the temperature of their body (thermoregulation), to protect their body, to attract mates and for identifying the species of bird.

Emu feathers

The feathers consist of keratin, which is what your fingernails are made from. The rachis is the hollow shaft at the center of the bird. The barbs are the thin branches connected to the shaft of the feather. The barbules are the smaller branches connected to the barbs. Collectively, the branches create a light source that gathers air for flying.

Ostrich feathers

The contour feathers are the feathers that cover the bird's body and contain the rachis and branches. The down feathers are the smaller feathers and can be found beneath the contour feathers. These feathers help to insulate the birds from cold weather.

Penguin feathers

WHICH BIRD HAS THE MOST FEATHERS?

Typically, the swan is considered to have the most feathers and a certain species of tundra swan have over 25,000 feathers. The average bird has only 1,000 to 2,000 feathers. Think about that the next time you see a beautiful swan.

White Tundra Swan

WHICH BIRD HAS THE FEWEST FEATHERS?

Feathers come in all shapes, sizes, and colors. While the smaller birds have smaller feathers, there are not as many feathers as there might be on a larger bird. The ruby-throated hummingbird has an average of 940 feathers.

Ruby-Throated Hummingbird

HOW DO THEY FLY?

Birds create lift beneath their wings by flapping them and using air pressure, similar to the way planes fly. Did you ever think about an airplane when you see a bird fly? Or think about a bird when you see an airplane in the air?

Peregrine Falcon (falco peregrinus) flying in the air

One of quickest birds is the peregrine falcon. When it is diving, it can reach a speed of over 100 miles per hour. While you have already learned about the feathers, they are also important to birds in providing them camouflage. Their hollow bones make them light enough to fly. If their bones were not hollow, they would be too heavy to fly.

A Peregrine Falcon perched on a stump. These birds are the fastest animals in the world.

Ostrich eggs

THEIR EGGS

Birds lay eggs that are hard-shelled. This shell keeps it from drying out and allows its parents to sit on their eggs during the incubation period. While their shells are hard, they do contain microscopic pores allowing for oxygen to pass through it to the baby inside and allows for the carbon dioxide to escape from the egg.

BIRD EMBRYO

Allantoic fluid
Embryo
Air cell
Yolk
Albumen
Amniotic liquid
Eggshell

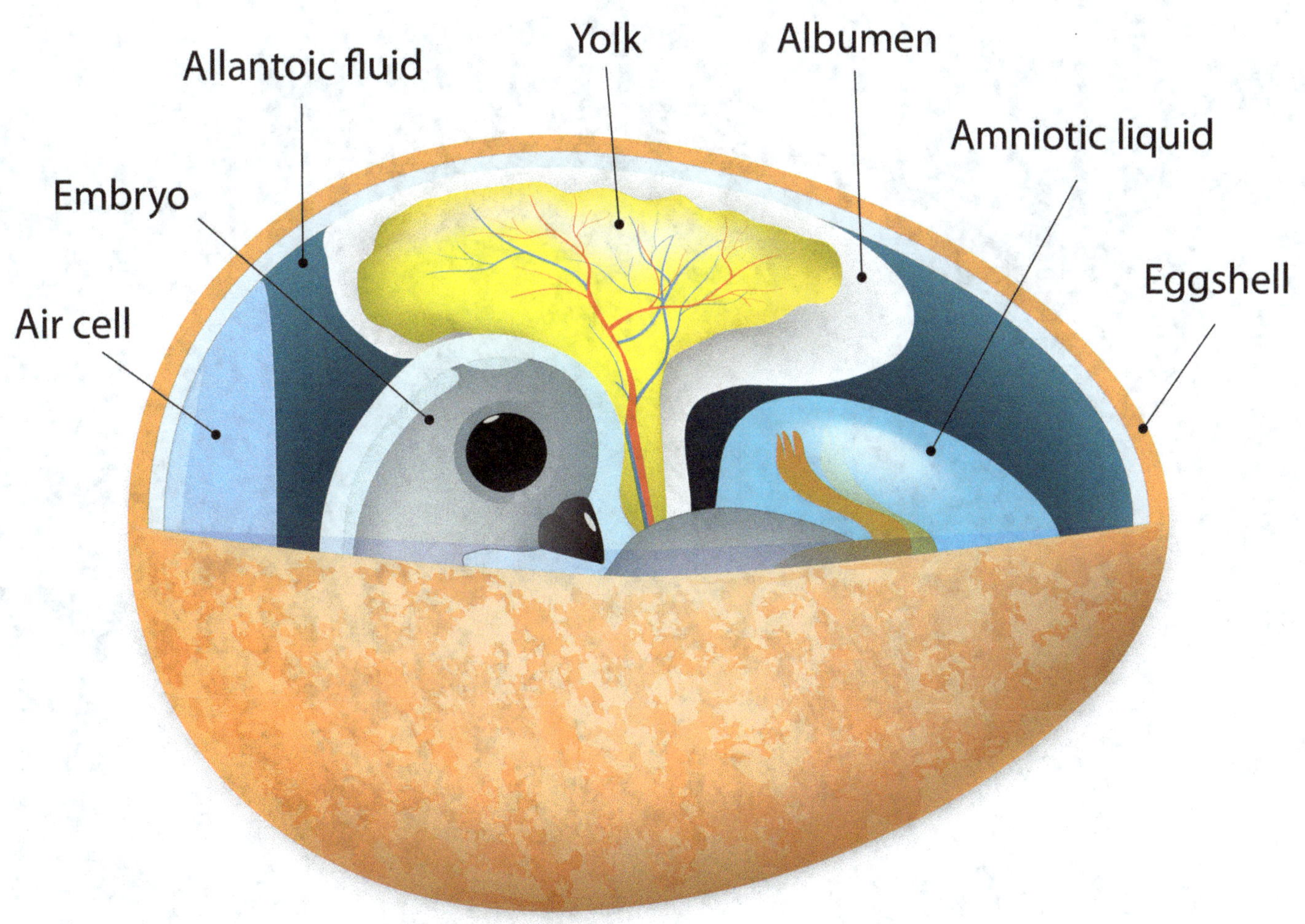

Their eggs can be found in varying textures, shapes, patterns, and colors. The patterns and colors on the eggs vary depending on how much camouflage they need. The shape of the egg is dependent upon where the nest is located. Most of the eggs are oval in shape. Eggs that are laid on a ledge needs a pointed end so that it will not roll off. The texture ranges from coarse (chicken) to smooth (hummingbird).

Robin's eggs and nest in their natural habitat.

There are many more species of flightless birds that we have not discussed. For additional information, go to your local library, research the internet, or ask questions of your teachers, family, and friends.

An illustration of a male and female Dodo Birds in a forest.
The dodo (Raphus cucullatus) is an extinct flightless bird that
was endemic to the island of Mauritius.

Visit
BABY PROFESSOR
EDUCATION KIDS
www.BabyProfessorBooks.com
to download Free Baby Professor eBooks
and view our catalog of new and exciting
Children's Books

www.ingramcontent.com/pod-product-compliance
Lightning Source LLC
Chambersburg PA
CBHW060222120726

48009CB00003B/111